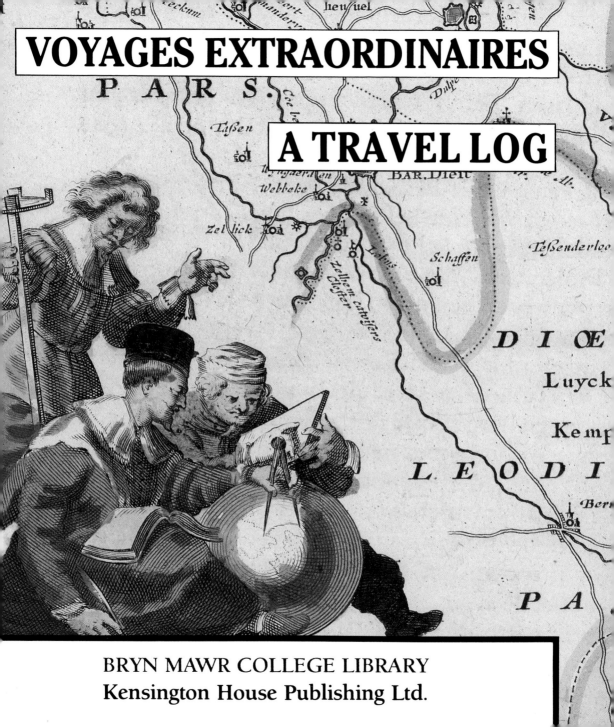

VOYAGES EXTRAORDINAIRES

A TRAVEL LOG

BRYN MAWR COLLEGE LIBRARY

Kensington House Publishing Ltd.

FRONT COVER:
Jules Verne, 1828-1905
L'Ile à Helice
Paris, 1895

ENDPAPERS:
Werner Rolevinck, 1425-1502
Fasciculus Temporum
Venice, 1481

TITLE PAGE:
Joan and Willem Blaeu
Grooten Atlas oft Wereltbeschryving
Amsterdam, 1664

First published in the United States in 1990
by Kensington House Publishing Ltd.
New York, U.S.A.
Images Copyright © Bryn Mawr College Library 1990.

KHM02   ISBN # 1-878518-21-6
Printed and Bound in Hong Kong.

Photography by Will Brown, Philadephia, PA
Calligraphy by Paula H. Struble, West Chester, PA

The Library Cloisters

The Library Cloisters
Vernon Howe Bailey, 1874-1953
Pencil drawing, circa 1910
Bryn Mawr College

Preface

Trips afield and journeys afar will provide you with opportunities to note your special itinerations in this Travel Log. Views from around the world, enlivening these pages throughout, are drawn from the Special Collections of Bryn Mawr College Library. Some of the originals, like the scene of Venice on the endpapers, are from fifteenth-century books; the other pictures are from the centuries following. Some came into the College's collections soon after its founding in 1885; the others have been added in the years since. All were chosen to entice and transport you to distant places, both in fact and in fancy.

The front cover, presenting our theme of *Voyages Extraordinaires*, is adapted from the binding of one of the captivating travel tales by Jules Verne. The early Dutch cartographers pictured on the title-page are eager to introduce you to the delights of plotting a course and detailing its outcome in the pages which follow.

Jotting down those "special things to remember" will provide opportunities for future moments of delight and recollection.

Travel well!

James Tanis
Director of Libraries
Bryn Mawr College

"Independence Hall"
John Rubens Smith, 1775-1849
Watercolor, 1829

Trip To _____

Date of departure: _____

Return on: _____

Arranged by: _____

Best time to visit: _____

Temperature range: _____

RECOMMENDATIONS

Sights to see: _____

_____

_____

_____

Local delicacies to taste: _____

Local wines to sample: _____

Items to buy: _____

_____

_____

Travel reading: _____

_____

Accommodations & Restaurants

Accommodation: _____

Tel.#: _____ Rate: _____

Comments: _____

_____

Restaurant: _____

Tel.#: _____

Specialties: _____

Comments: _____

Restaurant: _____

Tel.#: _____

Specialties: _____

Comments: _____

Restaurant: _____

Tel.#: _____

Specialties: _____

Comments: _____

_____

Accommodation: _____

Tel.#: _____ Rate: _____

Comments: _____

_____

Accommodation: _____

Tel.#: _____

Comments: _____

East Hampton, from the Church Belfry
Harry Fenn, 1838-1911
Picturesque America
New York, 1872-1874

Sights To See

_____

_____

_____

_____

_____

Places Visited

_____

_____

_____

_____

_____

_____

_____

_____

The President's House, Washington
Drawn by **H. Brown**
Engraved by Fenner, Sears & Co.
Hand-colored engraving, 1831

Journey To _____

Date of departure: _____

Return on: _____

Arranged by: _____

Best time to visit: _____

Temperature range: _____

RECOMMENDATIONS

Sights to see: _____

_____

_____

_____

Local delicacies to taste: _____

Local wines to sample: _____

Items to buy: _____

_____

_____

_____

Travel reading: _____

_____

_____

Accommodations

Accommodation: _____

Tel.#: _____ Rate: _____

Comments: _____

_____

Accommodation: _____

Tel.#: _____ Rate: _____

Comments: _____

_____

Accommodation: _____

Tel.#: _____ Rate: _____

Comments: _____

_____

Accommodation: _____

Tel.#: _____ Rate: _____

Comments: _____

_____

Accommodation: _____

Tel.#: _____ Rate: _____

Comments: _____

_____

"Proposal for Washington Monument"
*Morrison's Description of the Public Buildings and
Statues of Washington City.*
Washington, 1860

Restaurants

Restaurant: _____   Restaurant: _____

Tel.#: _____   Tel.#: _____

Specialties: _____   Specialties: _____

Comments: _____   Comments: _____

_____   _____

Restaurant: _____   Restaurant: _____

Tel.#: _____   Tel.#: _____

Specialties: _____   Specialties: _____

Comments: _____   Comments: _____

_____   _____

Restaurant: _____   Restaurant: _____

Tel.#: _____   Tel.#: _____

Specialties: _____   Specialties: _____

Comments: _____   Comments: _____

_____   _____

Restaurant: _____   Restaurant: _____

Tel.#: _____   Tel.#: _____

Specialties: _____   Specialties: _____

Comments: _____   Comments: _____

Sulphur Island
Basil Hall, 1788-1844
Account of a Voyage of Discovery
to the West Coast of Corea
London, 1818

Places Visited

Sights To See

_____

_____

_____

_____

_____

_____

_____

_____

_____

_____

"Cartouche for Beerings' Travels"
Jean Baptiste DuHalde, 1674-1743
A Description of the Empire of China.
London, 1738-1741

Special Things To Remember

"Vesuvius"
Sir William Hamilton, 1730-1803
Supplement to the Campi Phlegraei
Naples, 1779

Trip To _____

Date of departure: _____

Return on: _____

Arranged by: _____

Best time to visit: _____

Temperature range: _____

RECOMMENDATIONS

Sights to see: _____

_____

_____

_____

Local delicacies to taste: _____

Local wines to sample: _____

Items to buy: _____

_____

_____

Travel reading: _____

_____

_____

Accommodations & Restaurants

Accommodation: _____

Tel.#: _____ Rate: _____

Comments: _____

Restaurant: _____

Tel.#: _____

Specialties: _____

Comments: _____

Restaurant: _____

Tel.#: _____

Specialties: _____

Comments: _____

Accommodation: _____

Tel.#: _____ Rate: _____

Comments: _____

Accommodation: _____

Tel.#: _____

Specialties: _____

Comments: _____

Restaurant: _____

Tel.#: _____

Specialties: _____

Comments: _____

Pompeii, Strada di Mercurio
Photograph, circa 1890

Sights To See

_____
_____
_____
_____
_____

Places Visited

_____
_____
_____
_____
_____
_____
_____
_____

The Blue Egyptian Water-Lily
Robert John Thornton, 1768?-1837
The Temple of Flora
London, 1799

Journey To _____

Date of departure: _____

Return on: _____

Arranged by: _____

Best time to visit: _____

Temperature range: _____

RECOMMENDATIONS

Sights to see: _____

_____

_____

_____

Local delicacies to taste: _____

Local wines to sample: _____

Items to buy: _____

_____

_____

Travel reading: _____

_____

Accommodations

Accommodation: _____

Tel.#: _____ Rate: _____

Comments: _____

_____

Accommodation: _____

Tel.#: _____ Rate: _____

Comments: _____

_____

Accommodation: _____

Tel.#: _____ Rate: _____

Comments: _____

_____

Accommodation: _____

Tel.#: _____ Rate: _____

Comments: _____

_____

Accommodation: _____

Tel.#: _____ Rate: _____

Comments: _____

_____

Accommodation: _____

Tel.#: _____ Rate: _____

Comments: _____

_____

Ile de Phylae, Temple Hypéthre
Pascal Sébah
Photograph, circa 1880

Restaurants

Restaurant: _____

Tel.#: _____

Specialties: _____

Comments: _____
_____

Restaurant: _____

Tel.#: _____

Specialties: _____

Comments: _____
_____

Restaurant: _____

Tel.#: _____

Specialties: _____

Comments: _____
_____

Restaurant: _____

Tel.#: _____

Specialties: _____

Comments: _____

Restaurant: _____

Tel.#: _____

Specialties: _____

Comments: _____
_____

Restaurant: _____

Tel.#: _____

Specialties: _____

Comments: _____
_____

Restaurant: _____

Tel.#: _____

Specialties: _____

Comments: _____
_____

Restaurant: _____

Tel.#: _____

Specialties: _____

Comments: _____

Ancient Temples at Agrigentum
R. Bowyer, publisher
Hand-colored aquatint, 1809

Places Visited

Sights To See

_____

_____

_____

_____

_____

_____

_____

_____

_____

Mosque at Benares
Robert Elliot, fl. 1822
*Views of India, China, and on
the Shores of the Red Sea*
London, 1835

Special Things To Remember

Shāh Nāmeh (*The Book of Kings*)
Firdawsi, ca.935 - ca.1020
Persian miniature in 19th-century manuscript

Trip To _____

Date of departure: _____

Return on: _____

Arranged by: _____

Best time to visit: _____

Temperature range: _____

RECOMMENDATIONS

Sights to see: _____

_____

_____

_____

Local delicacies to taste: _____

Local wines to sample: _____

Items to buy: _____

_____

_____

Travel reading: _____

_____

Accommodations & Restaurants

Accommodation: _____

Tel.#: _____ Rate: _____

Comments: _____

Restaurant: _____

Tel.#: _____

Specialties: _____

Comments: _____

Restaurant: _____

Tel.#: _____

Specialties: _____

Comments: _____

Accommodation: _____

Tel.#: _____ Rate: _____

Comments: _____

Accommodation: _____

Tel.#: _____

Specialties: _____

Comments: _____

Restaurant: _____

Tel.#: _____

Specialties: _____

Comments: _____

A Mosque
Frederic Shoberl, 1775-1853, editor
The World in Miniature: Turkey
London, 1821

Sights To See

_____

_____

_____

_____

_____

Places Visited

_____

_____

_____

_____

_____

_____

_____

_____

Old Hastings: Christmas Eve, 1912
Albert Goodwin
Watercolor, 1912

Journey To _____

Date of departure: _____

Return on: _____

Arranged by: _____

Best time to visit: _____

Temperature range: _____

RECOMMENDATIONS

Sights to see: _____

_____

_____

_____

Local delicacies to taste: _____

Local wines to sample: _____

Items to buy: _____

_____

_____

Travel reading: _____

_____

_____

Accommodations

Accommodation: _____

Tel.#: _____ Rate: _____

Comments: _____

_____

Accommodation: _____

Tel.#: _____ Rate: _____

Comments: _____

_____

Accommodation: _____

Tel.#: _____ Rate: _____

Comments: _____

_____

Accommodation: _____

Tel.#: _____ Rate: _____

Comments: _____

_____

Accommodation: _____

Tel.#: _____ Rate: _____

Comments: _____

_____

Accommodation: _____

Tel.#: _____ Rate: _____

Comments: _____

_____

Regent's Canal
Thomas Hosmer Shepherd
Metropolitan Improvements, or,
London in the Nineteenth Century
London, 1827

Restaurants

Restaurant: _____

Tel.#: _____

Specialties: _____

Comments: _____
_____

Restaurant: _____

Tel.#: _____

Specialties: _____

Comments: _____
_____

Restaurant: _____

Tel.#: _____

Specialties: _____

Comments: _____
_____

Restaurant: _____

Tel.#: _____

Specialties: _____

Comments: _____

Restaurant: _____

Tel.#: _____

Specialties: _____

Comments: _____
_____

Restaurant: _____

Tel.#: _____

Specialties: _____

Comments: _____
_____

Restaurant: _____

Tel.#: _____

Specialties: _____

Comments: _____
_____

Restaurant: _____

Tel.#: _____

Specialties: _____

Comments: _____

"Puddle Porter"
Carl Jacob Lindström, 1800 - ca.1841
Costumi e Vestiture Napolitani
Naples, 1836

Places Visited

Sights To See

"Public Scribe"
Carl Jacob Lindström, 1880 - ca.1841
Costumi e Vestiture Napolitani
Naples, 1836

Special Things To Remember

The Ascent of Mont Blanc
George Baxter, 1804-1867
Oil-color print, circa 1855

Trip To _____

Date of departure: _____

Return on: _____

Arranged by: _____

Best time to visit: _____

Temperature range: _____

RECOMMENDATIONS

Sights to see: _____

_____

_____

_____

Local delicacies to taste: _____

Local wines to sample: _____

Items to buy: _____

_____

_____

Travel reading: _____

_____

Accommodations & Restaurants

Accommodation: _____

Tel.#: _____ Rate: _____

Comments: _____

Restaurant: _____

Tel.#: _____

Specialties: _____

Comments: _____

Restaurant: _____

Tel.#: _____

Specialties: _____

Comments: _____

Accommodation: _____

Tel.#: _____ Rate: _____

Comments: _____

Accommodation: _____

Tel.#: _____

Specialties: _____

Comments: _____

Restaurant: _____

Tel.#: _____

Specialties: _____

Comments: _____

Beset by the Ice
William Bradford, 1823-1892
The Arctic Regions
London, 1873

Sights To See

_____

_____

_____

_____

_____

Places Visited

_____

_____

_____

_____

_____

_____

_____

_____

_____

In the Omnibus
Mary Cassatt, 1844-1926
Color print with drypoint and
soft-ground etching, circa 1891

Journey To _____

Date of departure: _____

Return on: _____

Arranged by: _____

Best time to visit: _____

Temperature range: _____

RECOMMENDATIONS

Sights to see: _____

_____

_____

_____

Local delicacies to taste: _____

Local wines to sample: _____

Items to buy: _____

_____

_____

Travel reading: _____

_____

_____

Accommodations

Accommodation: _____

Tel.#: _____ Rate: _____

Comments: _____

_____

Accommodation: _____

Tel.#: _____ Rate: _____

Comments: _____

_____

Accommodation: _____

Tel.#: _____ Rate: _____

Comments: _____

_____

Accommodation: _____

Tel.#: _____ Rate: _____

Comments: _____

_____

Accommodation: _____

Tel.#: _____ Rate: _____

Comments: _____

_____

Accommodation: _____

Tel.#: _____ Rate: _____

Comments: _____

_____

S.S. Champlain Cabin Class Deck Plans
New York, 1936

Restaurants

Restaurant: _____

Tel.#: _____

Specialties: _____

Comments: _____
_____

Restaurant: _____

Tel.#: _____

Specialties: _____

Comments: _____
_____

Restaurant: _____

Tel.#: _____

Specialties: _____

Comments: _____
_____

Restaurant: _____

Tel.#: _____

Specialties: _____

Comments: _____

Restaurant: _____

Tel.#: _____

Specialties: _____

Comments: _____
_____

Restaurant: _____

Tel.#: _____

Specialties: _____

Comments: _____
_____

Restaurant: _____

Tel.#: _____

Specialties: _____

Comments: _____
_____

Restaurant: _____

Tel.#: _____

Specialties: _____

Comments: _____

Crossing the Line
George Cruikshank, 1792-1878
Matthew Henry Barker
Greenwich Hospital: A Series of Naval Sketches
London, 1826

Places Visited

Sights To See

_____

_____

_____

_____

_____

_____

_____

_____

_____

_____

"Methoni in the Peloponnisos"
Bernhard von Breydenbach
Die heyligen Reyssen
Mainz, 1488

Special Things To Remember

"The Pagoda"
William Alexander, 1767-1816
The Costume of China
London, 1805

Trip To _____

Date of departure: _____

Return on: _____

Arranged by: _____

Best time to visit: _____

Temperature range: _____

RECOMMENDATIONS

Sights to see: _____

_____

_____

_____

Local delicacies to taste: _____

Local wines to sample: _____

Items to buy: _____

_____

_____

Travel reading: _____

_____

Accommodations & Restaurants

Accommodation: _____

Tel.#:_____Rate:_____

Comments: _____

Restaurant:_____

Tel.#:_____

Specialties:_____

Comments: _____

Restaurant: _____

Tel.#: _____

Specialties:_____

Comments: _____

Accommodation: _____

Tel.#:_____Rate:_____

Comments: _____

Accommodation: _____

Tel.#: _____

Specialties:_____

Comments: _____

Restaurant: _____

Tel.#: _____

Specialties:_____

Comments: _____

A Curious Chinese Vessel
Edward Cavendish Drake
*A New Universal Collection of Authentic
and Entertaining Voyages*
London, 1768

Sights To See

_____

_____

_____

_____

_____

Places Visited

_____

_____

_____

_____

_____

_____

_____

_____

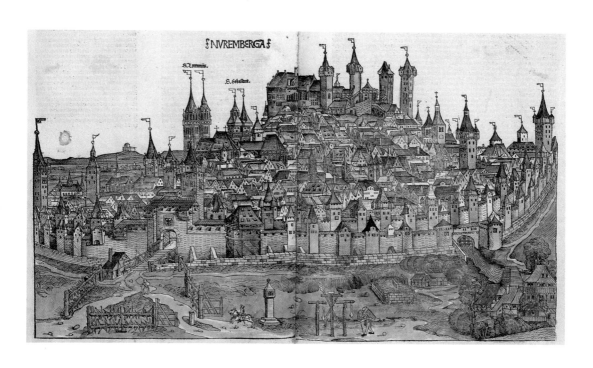

"Nuremberg, 1493"
Hartmann Schedel, 1440-1514
Liber Cronicarum

Journey To _____

Date of departure: _____

Return on: _____

Arranged by: _____

Best time to visit: _____

Temperature range: _____

RECOMMENDATIONS

Sights to see: _____

_____

_____

_____

Local delicacies to taste: _____

Local wines to sample: _____

Items to buy: _____

_____

_____

Travel reading: _____

_____

Accommodations

Accommodation: _____

Tel.#: _____ Rate: _____

Comments: _____

_____

Accommodation: _____

Tel.#: _____ Rate: _____

Comments: _____

_____

Accommodation: _____

Tel.#: _____ Rate: _____

Comments: _____

_____

Accommodation: _____

Tel.#: _____ Rate: _____

Comments: _____

_____

Accommodation: _____

Tel.#: _____ Rate: _____

Comments: _____

_____

Accommodation: _____

Tel.#: _____ Rate: _____

Comments: _____

_____

"The Fool Bears the World"
Sebastian Brant, 1458-1521
Das Narrenschiff
Basel, 1498

Restaurants

Restaurant: _____

Tel.#: _____

Specialties: _____

Comments: _____

_____

Restaurant: _____

Tel.#: _____

Specialties: _____

Comments: _____

_____

Restaurant: _____

Tel.#: _____

Specialties: _____

Comments: _____

_____

Restaurant: _____

Tel.#: _____

Specialties: _____

Comments: _____

Restaurant: _____

Tel.#: _____

Specialties: _____

Comments: _____

_____

Restaurant: _____

Tel.#: _____

Specialties: _____

Comments: _____

_____

Restaurant: _____

Tel.#: _____

Specialties: _____

Comments: _____

_____

Restaurant: _____

Tel.#: _____

Specialties: _____

Comments: _____

The Horse Shoe Fall, Niagara - with the Tower
William Henry Bartlett, 1809-1854
Hand-colored engraving, 1837

Places Visited

Sights To See

_____

_____

_____

_____

_____

_____

_____

_____

Fisher and the Bear
George W. Holley
Niagara
New York, 1872

Special Things To Remember

"Castle of Gutenfels"
Album of Rhine Views
Hand-painted print, circa 1850

Trip To _____

Date of departure: _____

Return on: _____

Arranged by: _____

Best time to visit: _____

Temperature range: _____

RECOMMENDATIONS

Sights to see: _____

_____

_____

_____

Local delicacies to taste: _____

Local wines to sample: _____

Items to buy: _____

_____

_____

Travel reading: _____

_____

Accommodations & Restaurants

Accommodation: _____

Tel.#: _____ Rate: _____

Comments: _____

_____

Restaurant: _____

Tel.#: _____

Specialties: _____

Comments: _____

Restaurant: _____

Tel.#: _____

Specialties: _____

Comments: _____

Restaurant: _____

Tel.#: _____

Specialties: _____

Comments: _____

_____

Accommodation: _____

Tel.#: _____ Rate: _____

Comments: _____

_____

Accommodation: _____

Tel.#: _____

Comments: _____

Josefsplatz
Maximilian Liebenwein
Alt-Wiener Bauten-Kalender
Vienna, 1911

Sights To See

_____

_____

_____

_____

_____

Places Visited

_____

_____

_____

_____

_____

_____

_____

_____

"Medieval Travellers"
Book of Hours
Flanders, circa 1440

Journey To _____

Date of departure: _____

Return on: _____

Arranged by: _____

Best time to visit: _____

Temperature range: _____

RECOMMENDATIONS

Sights to see: _____

_____

_____

_____

Local delicacies to taste: _____

Local wines to sample: _____

Items to buy: _____

_____

_____

Travel reading: _____

_____

Accommodations

Accommodation: _____

Tel.#: _____ Rate: _____

Comments: _____

_____

Accommodation: _____

Tel.#: _____ Rate: _____

Comments: _____

_____

Accommodation: _____

Tel.#: _____ Rate: _____

Comments: _____

_____

Accommodation: _____

Tel.#: _____ Rate: _____

Comments: _____

_____

Accommodation: _____

Tel.#: _____ Rate: _____

Comments: _____

_____

Accommodation: _____

Tel.#: _____ Rate: _____

Comments: _____

_____

"Windmills of Amsterdam"
Peter Schenk, 1661-1715
Views of Amsterdam
Amsterdam, circa 1700

Restaurants

Restaurant: _____

Tel.#: _____

Specialties: _____

Comments: _____
_____

Restaurant: _____

Tel.#: _____

Specialties: _____

Comments: _____
_____

Restaurant: _____

Tel.#: _____

Specialties: _____

Comments: _____
_____

Restaurant: _____

Tel.#: _____

Specialties: _____

Comments: _____

Restaurant: _____

Tel.#: _____

Specialties: _____

Comments: _____
_____

Restaurant: _____

Tel.#: _____

Specialties: _____

Comments: _____
_____

Restaurant: _____

Tel.#: _____

Specialties: _____

Comments: _____
_____

Restaurant: _____

Tel.#: _____

Specialties: _____

Comments: _____

The Castle Geyser
Thomas Moran, 1837-1926
Ferdinand Vandeveer Hayden
The Yellowstone National Park
Boston, 1876

Places Visited

Sights To See

Big Trees—Mariposa Grove
James David Smillie, 1833-1909
Picturesque America
New York, 1872-1874

Special Things To Remember

"Macalister Goes To Canada"
Robert Ronald McIan
James Logan
The Clans of the Scottish Highlands
London, 1845-1847

Trip To _____

Date of departure: _____

Return on: _____

Arranged by: _____

Best time to visit: _____

Temperature range: _____

RECOMMENDATIONS

Sights to see: _____

_____

_____

_____

Local delicacies to taste: _____

Local wines to sample: _____

Items to buy: _____

_____

_____

Travel reading: _____

_____

_____

Accommodations & Restaurants

Accommodation: _____

Tel.#: _____ Rate: _____

Comments: _____
_____

Restaurant: _____

Tel.#: _____

Specialties: _____

Comments: _____

Restaurant: _____

Tel.#: _____

Specialties: _____

Comments: _____

Accommodation: _____

Tel.#: _____ Rate: _____

Comments: _____
_____

Accommodation: _____

Tel.#: _____

Specialties: _____

Comments: _____

Restaurant: _____

Tel.#: _____

Specialties: _____

Comments: _____

Her Majesty at Balmoral
George Baxter, 1804-1867
Oil color print, circa 1850

Sights To See

_____

_____

_____

_____

_____

Places Visited

_____

_____

_____

_____

_____

_____

_____

_____

_____

"The Village"
William John Burchell, 1782?-1863
Travels in the Interior of Southern Africa
London, 1822-1824

Journey To _____

Date of departure: _____

Return on: _____

Arranged by: _____

Best time to visit: _____

Temperature range: _____

RECOMMENDATIONS

Sights to see: _____

_____

_____

_____

Local delicacies to taste: _____

Local wines to sample: _____

Items to buy: _____

_____

_____

Travel reading: _____

_____

Accommodations

Accommodation: _____

Tel.#: _____ Rate: _____

Comments: _____

_____

Accommodation: _____

Tel.#: _____ Rate: _____

Comments: _____

_____

Accommodation: _____

Tel.#: _____ Rate: _____

Comments: _____

_____

Accommodation: _____

Tel.#: _____ Rate: _____

Comments: _____

_____

Accommodation: _____

Tel.#: _____ Rate: _____

Comments: _____

_____

Accommodation: _____

Tel.#: _____ Rate: _____

Comments: _____

"Wooden Fanti Doll"
Tribal African art

Restaurants

Restaurant: _____

Tel.#: _____

Specialties: _____

Comments: _____

_____

Restaurant: _____

Tel.#: _____

Specialties: _____

Comments: _____

_____

Restaurant: _____

Tel.#: _____

Specialties: _____

Comments: _____

_____

Restaurant: _____

Tel.#: _____

Specialties: _____

Comments: _____

Restaurant: _____

Tel.#: _____

Specialties: _____

Comments: _____

_____

Restaurant: _____

Tel.#: _____

Specialties: _____

Comments: _____

_____

Restaurant: _____

Tel.#: _____

Specialties: _____

Comments: _____

_____

Restaurant: _____

Tel.#: _____

Specialties: _____

Comments: _____

Lady in a Car
Frederic Shoberl, 1775-1853, editor
The World in Miniature: Japan
London, 1823

Places Visited

Sights To See

_____

_____

_____

_____

_____

_____

_____

_____

_____

_____

The Nana Sahib with His Escort
Charles Ball
The History of the Indian Mutiny
London, 1858-1859

Special Things To Remember

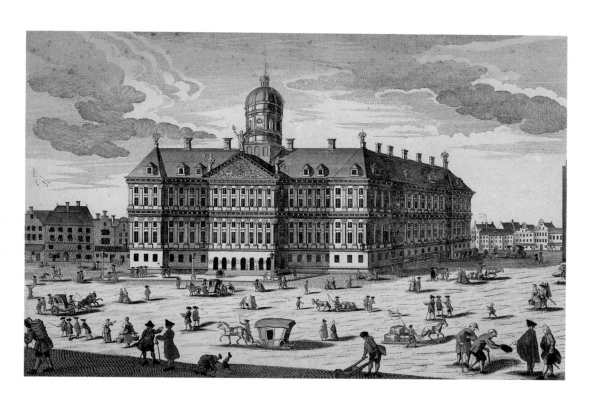

't Stadhuys van Amsteldam
P. van Blankaert
Hand-colored mirror print, circa 1790

Trip To _____

Date of departure: _____

Return on: _____

Arranged by: _____

Best time to visit: _____

Temperature range: _____

RECOMMENDATIONS

Sights to see: _____

_____

_____

_____

Local delicacies to taste: _____

Local wines to sample: _____

Items to buy: _____

_____

_____

Travel reading: _____

_____

_____

Accommodations & Restaurants

Accommodation: _____

Tel.#: _____ Rate: _____

Comments: _____

_____

Restaurant: _____

Tel.#: _____

Specialties: _____

Comments: _____

Restaurant: _____

Tel.#: _____

Specialties: _____

Comments: _____

Restaurant: _____

Tel.#: _____

Specialties: _____

Comments: _____

Accommodation: _____

Tel.#: _____ Rate: _____

Comments: _____

_____

Accommodation: _____

Tel.#: _____

Comments: _____

Lady of French Friburg
Frederic Shoberl, 1775-1853, editor
The World in Miniature: Switzerland
London, circa 1821

Sights To See

_____

_____

_____

_____

_____

Places Visited

_____

_____

_____

_____

_____

_____

_____

_____

Important Telephone Numbers

NAME	NUMBER

"Photographer's Wagon"
William Henry Jackson, 1843-1942
Photograph, circa 1875

New Friends

Name: _____

Address: _____

_____

Where Met: _____

Tel. No.: _____

Name: _____

Address: _____

_____

Where Met: _____

Tel. No.: _____

Name: _____

Address: _____

_____

Where Met: _____

Tel. No.: _____

Name: _____

Address: _____

_____

Where Met: _____

Tel. No.: _____

Name: _____

Address: _____

_____

Where Met: _____

Tel. No.: _____

Name: _____

Address: _____

_____

Where Met: _____

Tel. No.: _____

Name: _____

Address: _____

_____

Where Met: _____

Tel. No.: _____

Name: _____

Address: _____

_____

Where Met: _____

Tel. No.: _____